The Voice of God is an imprint of As I Grow Publishing
Ledon Studios LLC, Richmond, VA
AsIGrow.org
SilviaLedon@AsIGrow.org

Edited by Tamara Rittershaus
Photography by Amanda Miles Photography

Paperback ISBN: 979-8-9895151-0-3
Hardcover ISBN: 979-8-9895151-1-0
E-Book ISBN: 979-8-9895151-2-7
Spanish Version, La Voz de Dios ISBN: 979-8-9895151-5-8

Library of Congress : LCCN 2023920916

Asigrow.org

The Voice of God

Written by Silvia Ledon

Illustrated by Diana Canales Rojas

As I Grow Publishers

Thank You!

Juan, my best friend:

I couldn't have published this book without your love, your belief in me, and your unwavering support.

I love you forever.

Mom:

Our conversations have been life-giving. You have been my biggest fan, and I am eternally grateful for you.

Lizette, Gabriel, Daniel, and Elise:

You have inspired me in more ways than you will ever know.

Memories of you discovering God as you were growing up, are the biggest source of joy in my life.

Friends who cheered me along, proofread, gave me input, made suggestions, and showered me with encouraging words.

I am divinely blessed by you.

For Nehemiah and Graham

May you always hear God's
gentle voice in the stillness of
your hearts.
S.L

For Julian

May curiosity and joy open
your heart to your spiritual
path and God's call.
D.C.

The Voice
Of God

God is always speaking to me.
God's voice is not like the voice of a person.
I don't need my ears to hear it.

When I pay attention, I recognize it.

Sometimes I hear God in
the beautiful world I live in.
I notice all that God has made:
mountains,
trees,
colorful flowers,
animals in the wild,
and stars in the sky.

When I think of how amazing God is my heart feels full and grateful.

That is when I know God is speaking.

Sometimes I hear God through another person. When someone hugs me or tells me "I love you" or when someone is kind towards me, I feel goodness all around me.

That is when I know God is speaking.

Sometimes I hear God in silence.
Being still and patient
can help me understand things
about God,
about others,
about myself.

That is when I know God is speaking.

God's voice is not harsh.
It is gentle.
It is not scary.
It is kind.

When I feel loved, safe, and understood
I know God is speaking.

When I am happy or when I am sad,
when I am angry or when I am calm,
when I play or when I sleep,
God is always with me.

No matter where I am, I can pay attention
and hear the voice of God.

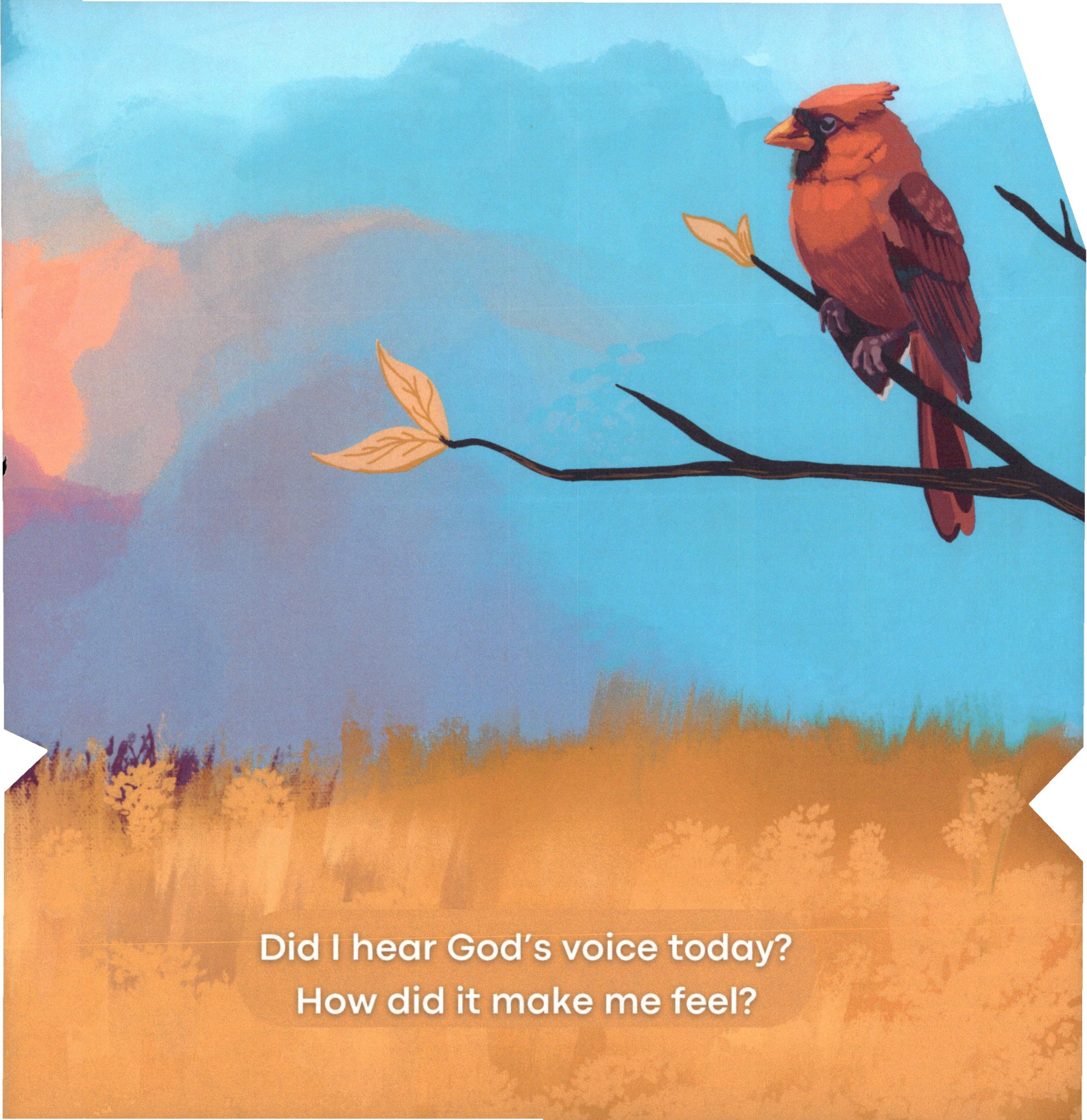

Did I hear God's voice today?
How did it make me feel?

I wonder how I will hear
the voice of God tomorrow.

Let's talk about it.

There are some things God is always saying.

Which of these have you heard deep in your heart lately?

You are never alone.

My love for you is bigger than the whole world.

Your heart is safe with me.

I created you to be just like you are.

You are beautiful.

I see you and understand you.

You are my precious child.

I am with you, as close as the air you breathe.

You bring me so much joy.

I love it when you think of me.

I hear you.

Download free journal printable pages.
Scan here

As I Grow

Note from the author

This book draws its inspiration from conversations shared with my dearest friend, Becky, at the tender age of four. In nature's canvas, I discovered the divine thumbprint, which anchored my soul forever.

Note from the Illustrator

The illustrations were woven together with a magical tapestry of hundreds of pixels, bounded together with much enthusiasm and conveyed with tender care for the viewers to enjoy.